ॐ

Sanskrit alphabet (Devanāgarī) Study Book

Volume 1
Single letters

Medhā Michika

All profit from the sales of this book goes towards the activities initiated by Śrī Pūjya Svamī Dayānanda Sarasvatī.

Electronic version of this book is available at:
Arsha Avinash Foundation
www.arshaavinash.in

Printed version of this book is available at:
Arsha Vidya Gurukulam, Coimbatore, TN, India
www.arshavidya.in
Swami Dayananda Ashram, Rishikesh, UK, India
www.dayananda.org
Arsha Vidya Gurukulam, Saylorsburg, PA, USA
www.arshavidya.org
CreateSpace
www.createspace.com (Search by "medha michika")
Amazon of your country
www.amazon.com etc. (Search by "medha michika")

Table of contents

= Introduction =

= Vowels at the beginning of word =

= Consonants =

ॐ

om

शुक्लाम्बरधरं विष्णुं शशिवर्णं चतुर्भुजम् ।
प्रसन्नवदनं ध्यायेत् सर्वविघ्नोपशान्तये ॥

śuklāmbaradharaṃ viṣṇuṃ śaśivarṇaṃ caturbhujam ।
prasannavadanaṃ dhyāyet sarvavighnopaśāntaye ।।

सरस्वति नमस्तुभ्यं वरदे कामरूपिणि ।
विद्यारम्भं करिष्यामि सिद्धिर्भवतु मे सदा ॥

sarasvati namastubhyaṃ varade kāmarūpiṇi ।
vidyārambhaṃ kariṣyāmi siddhirbhavatu me sadā ।।

ॐ शान्तिः शान्तिः शान्तिः ॥

om śāntiḥ śāntiḥ śāntiḥ ।।

प्रयत्नाः (Efforts)	स्पृष्टाः (Contact)					ईषत्स्पृष्टाः (Slightly contact)	ईषद्विवृताः (Slightly open)		विवृताः (Open)
स्थानानि (Places)	Hard		Soft				Hard	Soft	स्वराः
वर्णाः (Types of sound)	अल्पप्राणाः (Non-asp.)	महाप्राणाः (Aspirate)	अल्पप्राणाः (Non-asp.)	महाप्राणाः (Aspirate)	अल्पप्राणाः (Non-aspirate)		महाप्राणाः (Aspirate)		
	1st of the class	2nd of the class	3rd of the class	4th of the class	5th / (Nasals)	Semi vowels	Sibilants		Vowels
कण्ठः Throat (कण्ठ्याः Gutturals)	क ka	ख kha	ग ga	घ gha	ङ ṅa			ह ha	अ * / आ a / ā
तालु Palate (तालव्याः Palatals)	च ca	छ cha	ज ja	झ jha	ञ ña	य ya	श śa		इ / ई i / ī
मूर्धा Roof (मूर्धन्याः Cerebrals)	ट ṭa	ठ ṭha	ड ḍa	ढ ḍha	ण ṇa	र ra	ष ṣa		ऋ / ॠ ṛ / ṝ
दन्ताः Teeth (दन्त्याः Dentals)	त ta	थ tha	द da	ध dha	न na	ल la	स sa		ऌ ḷ
ओष्ठौ Lips (ओष्ठ्याः Labials)	प pa	फ pha	ब ba	भ bha	म ma	व * va			उ / ऊ u / ū

कण्ठतालु – ए e, ऐ ai

नासिका – अं ṁ (अनुस्वारः)

* Effort of अ – संवृतः

कण्ठोष्ठम् – ओ o, औ au

कण्ठः – अः ḥ (विसर्जनीयः)

** दन्तोष्ठम् – व va

Chapter 1.
Vowels at the beginning of a word

Legend: m. = masculine; f. = feminine; n. = neuter; ind. = indeclinable; a. = adjective

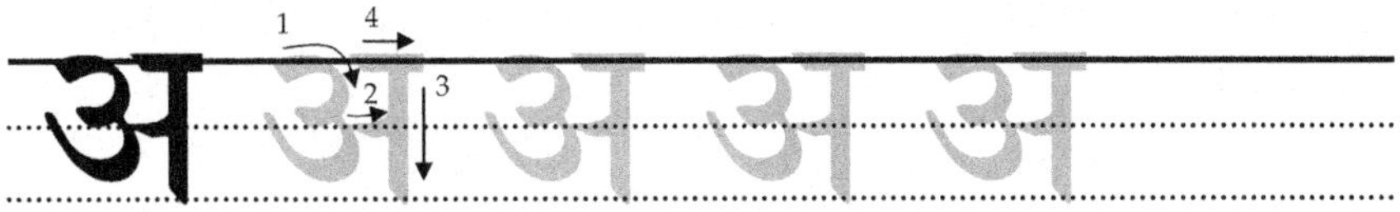

a

अथ	अजः
atha	ajaḥ
(ind.)	(m.)
now	brahman

ā

आत्मा	आकाशः
ātmā	ākāśaḥ
(m.)	(m.)
self	space

इ

i

इदम्	इह
idam	iha
(n.)	(ind.)
this	here

ई

ī

ईशः	ईश्वरः
īśaḥ	īśvaraḥ
(m.)	(m.)
lord	lord

उ

u

उदकम्	उमा
udakam	umā
(n.)	(f.)
water	pārvatī

ऊ

ū

ऊरुः	ऊर्ध्वम्
ūruḥ	ūrdhvam
(m.)	(ind.)
thigh	upward

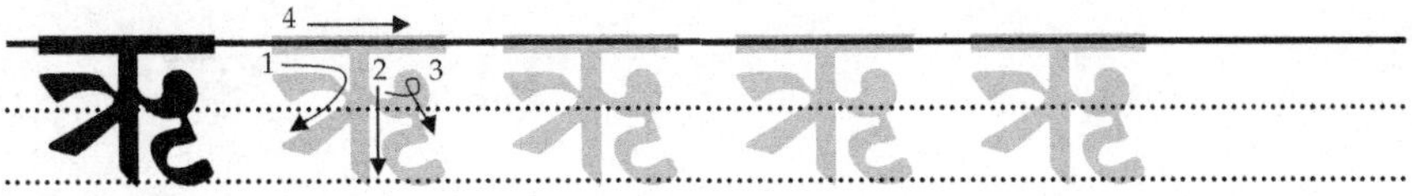

ṛ

ऋतम्　ऋक्

ṛtam　ṛk

(ind.)　(f.)

truly　mantra

ṝ

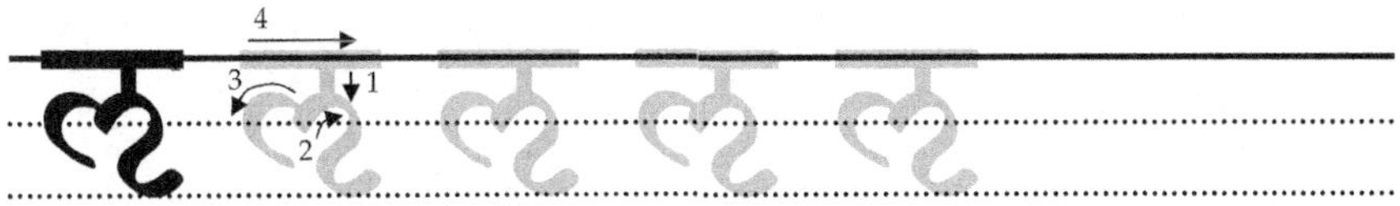

ḷ

There is no long ऌ sound.

ए

e

एव	एषः
eva	eṣaḥ
(ind.)	(m.)
only, just	this

ऐ

ai

ऐक्यम्	ऐश्वर्यम्
aikyam	aiśvaryam
(n.)	(n.)
oneness	lordship

ओ

o

ओम्	ओष्ठः
om	oṣṭhaḥ
(ind.)	(m.)
om	lip

औ

au

औषधिः	औष्ण्यम्
auṣadhiḥ	auṣṇyam
(f.)	(n.)
herb	heat

Chapter 2.
Consonants followed by vowels

क्+अ=क　　क्+अ=क

k + a = ka　　k + a = ka

क्+आ=का　　क्+आ=का

k + ā = kā　　k + ā = kā

क्+इ=कि　　क्+इ=कि

k + i = ki　　k + i = ki

क् + ई = की	क् + ई = की
k + ī = kī	k + ī = kī
क् + उ = कु	क् + उ = कु
k + u = ku	k + u = ku
क् + ऊ = कू	क् + ऊ = कू
k + ū = kū	k + ū = kū
क् + ऋ = कृ	क् + ऋ = कृ
k + ṛ = kṛ	k + ṛ = kṛ
क् + ॠ = कॄ	क् + ॠ = कॄ
k + ṝ = kṝ	k + ṝ = kṝ
क् + ए = के	क् + ए = के
k + e = ke	k + e = ke

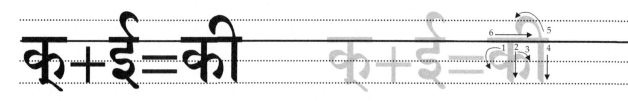

क्+ऐ=कै क्+ऐ=कै

k + ai = kai   k + ai = kai

क्+ओ=को क्+ओ=को

k + o = ko   k + o = ko

क्+औ=कौ क्+औ=कौ

k + au = kau   k + au = kau

क क क क क

ka

कथा
kathā
(f.)
story

कमलम्
kamalam
(n.)
lotus

का का का का का

kā

काकः
kākaḥ
(m.)
crow

कालः
kālaḥ
(m.)
time

कि कि कि कि कि

ki

किम्
kim
(n.)
what

किरणः
kiraṇaḥ
(m.)
ray of light

की की की की की

kī

कीटः
kīṭaḥ
(m.)
warm

कीर्तिः
kīrtiḥ
(f.)
fame

कु कु कु कु कु

ku

कुमारः kumāraḥ (m.) young boy

कुलम् kulam (n.) family

कू कू कू कू कू

kū

कूटस्थ kūṭastha (a.) unchange-able

कूपः kūpaḥ (m.) well

कृ कृ कृ कृ कृ

kṛ

कृपा kṛpā (f.) compassion

कृष्णः kṛṣṇaḥ (m.) name of god

कॄ कॄ कॄ कॄ कॄ

kṝ

के के के के के

ke

केशवः — keśavaḥ — (m.) name of kṛṣṇa

केवल — kevala — (a.) only

कै कै कै कै कै

kai

कैलासः — kailāsaḥ — (m.) name of a holy place

कैवल्यम् — kaivalyam — (n.) exclusiveness

को को को को को

ko

कोटिः — koṭiḥ — (f.) crore

कोशः — kośaḥ — (m.) sheath

कौ कौ कौ कौ कौ

kau

कौमुदी — kaumudī — (f.) moonlight

कौरवः — kauravaḥ — (m.) descendant of Kurus

ख ख ख ख ख

kha

खम्
kham
(n.)
sky

खगः
khagaḥ
(m.)
bird

खा खा खा खा खा

khā

खाद्य
khādya
(a.)
edible

खानम्
khānam
(n.)
digging

खि खि खि खि खि

khi

खिन्न
khinna
(a.)
distressed

खे खे खे खे खे

khe

खेदः
khedaḥ
(m.)
pain

खेला
khelā
(f.)
sport

ग ग ग ग ग

ga

गगनम् गणेशः

gaganam ganeśaḥ

(n.) (m.)

sky name of god

गा गा गा गा गा

gā

गायकः गायत्री

gāyakaḥ gāyatrī

(m.) (f.)

singer name of goddess

गि गि गि गि गि

gi

गिरिः गिर्

giriḥ gir

(m.) (f.)

hill word

गी गी गी गी गी

gī

गीता

gītā

(f.)

name of a sacred scripture

गु गु गु गु गु

gu

गुरुः
guruḥ
(m.)
teacher

गुणः
guṇaḥ
(m.)
quality

गू गू गू गू गू

gū

गूढ
gūḍha
(a.)
hidden

गृ गृ गृ गृ गृ

gṛ

गृहम्
gṛham
(n.)
house

गृहस्थः
gṛhasthaḥ
(m.)
householder

गे गे गे गे गे

ge

गेयम्
geyam
(n.)
song

गेहम्
geham
(n.)
house

गो गो गो गो गो

go

गोचरः
gocaraḥ
(m.)
range

गोपालः
gopālaḥ
(m.)
cowherd

गौ गौ गौ गौ गौ

gau

गौः
gauḥ
(f.)
cow

गौरी
gaurī
(f.)
name of Pārvatī

घ घ घ घ घ

1 2 3

gha

घटः
ghaṭaḥ
(m.)
pot

घनः
ghanaḥ
(m.)
cloud

घा घा घा घा घा

ghā

घातकः
ghātakaḥ
(m.)
slayer

घि घि घि घि घि

ghi

घृ घृ घृ घृ घृ

ghṛ

घृतम्
ghṛtam
(n.)
ghee

घु घु घु घु घु

ghu

रघुः   लघु
raghuḥ   laghu
(m.)   (a.)
name of a   small, light
king

घो घो घो घो घो

gho

घोर   घोषः
ghora   ghoṣaḥ
(a.)   (m.)
violent   proclamation

ङ ङ ङ ङ ङ

ṅa

ङि ङि ङि ङि ङि

ṅi

ङे ङे ङे ङे ङे

ṅe

ङो ङो ङो ङो ङो

ṅo

च च च च च

ca

चक्रम् cakram (n.) wheel

चन्द्रः candraḥ (m.) moon

चा चा चा चा चा

cā

चारु cāru (a.) pleasant

चापम् cāpam (n.) bow

चि चि चि चि चि

ci

चित्तम् cittam (n.) mind

चिर cira (a.) long time

ची ची ची ची ची

cī

चु चु चु चु चु

cu

प्रचुर pracura (a.) abundant

चुम्बः cumbaḥ (m.) kiss

चू चू चू चू चू

cū

चूर्णम् cūrṇam (n.) powder

चूडा cūḍā (f.) crest

चे चे चे चे चे

ce

चेतनः cetanaḥ (m.) conscious being

चेष्टा ceṣṭā (f.) movement

चै चै चै चै चै

cai

चैतन्यम् caitanyam (n.) consciousness

चैत्रः caitraḥ (m.) name of a month

चो चो चो चो चो

co

चोदना   चोरः

codanā   coraḥ

(f.)   (m.)

inspiration   thief

चौ चौ चौ चौ चौ

cau

चौरः

cauraḥ

(m.)

thief

छ छ छ छ छ

cha

छत्रः   छन्दस्

chatraḥ   chandas

(m.)   (n.)

umbrella   the Veda

छा छा छा छा छा

chā

छाया   छात्रः

chāyā   chātraḥ

(f.)   (m.)

shadow   pupil

छि छि छि छि छि

chi

छिन्न
chinna
(a.)
torn

छिद्रम्
chidram
(n.)
hole

छे छे छे छे छे

che

छेदनम्
chedanam
(n.)
cutting

ज ज ज ज ज

ja

जगत्
jagat
(n.)
universe

जलम्
jalam
(n.)
water

जा जा जा जा जा

jā

जातिः
jātiḥ
(f.)
class

जातु
jātu
(ind.)
ever

जि जि जि जि जि

ji

जिह्वा   जिज्ञासुः

jihvā   jijñāsuḥ

(f.)   (m.)

tongue   one who desires to know

जी जी जी जी जी

jī

जीवः   जीर्ण

jīvaḥ   jīrṇa

(m.)   (a.)

individual   old

जु जु जु जु जु

ju

जुष्ट   जुगुप्सा

juṣṭa   jugupsā

(a.)   (f.)

gratified   disgust

जू जू जू जू जू

jū

जूटः

jūṭaḥ

(m.)

matted hair

जृ जृ जृ जृ जृ

jṛ

जृभः
jṛbhaḥ
(m.)
yawning

जृभणम्
jṛbhaṇam
(n.)
yawning

जे जे जे जे जे

je

जेता
jetā
(m.)
winner

जै जै जै जै जै

jai

जैमिनिः
jaiminiḥ
(m.)
name of a teacher

जैनः
jainaḥ
(m.)
name of a sage

जो जो जो जो जो

jo

जोषम्
joṣam
(n.)
happiness

झ झ झ झ झ

jha

झषः	झटिति
jhaṣaḥ	jhaṭiti
(m.)	(ind.)
fish	quickly

झा झा झा झा झा

jha

झाटिका

jhāṭikā
(f.)
jasmine

ञ ञ ञ ञ ञ

ña

ञा ञा ञा ञा ञा

ñā

ट ट ट ट ट

ṭa

कूटः kūṭaḥ (m.) anvil

घटः ghaṭaḥ (m.) pot

टि टि टि टि टि

ṭi

टिप्पणी ṭippaṇī (f.) footnote

टी टी टी टी टी

ṭī

टीका ṭīkā (f.) commentary

टु टु टु टु टु

ṭu

टे टे टे टे टे

ṭe

टो टो टो टो टो

ṭo

ठ ठ ठ ठ ठ

ṭha

पीठम् pīṭham (m.) seat

पाठः pāṭhaḥ (m.) reading

ठा ठा ठा ठा ठा

ṭhā

पीठा pīṭhā (f.) seat

निष्ठा niṣṭhā (f.) firmness

ठि ठि ठि ठि ठि

ṭhi

पठित
paṭhita
(a.)
recited

कठिन
kaṭhina
(a.)
hard

ठी ठी ठी ठी ठी

ṭhī

पीठी
pīṭhī
(f.)
seat

षष्ठी
ṣaṣṭhī
(f.)
sixth

ठु ठु ठु ठु ठु

ṭhu

सुष्ठु
suṣṭhu
(ind.)
well

कठुर
kaṭhura
(a.)
hard

ठृ ठृ ठृ ठृ ठृ

ṭhṛ

ठे ठे ठे ठे ठे

ṭhe

अनुष्ठेय

anuṣṭheya

(a.)

object to be performed

ठो ठो ठो ठो ठो

ṭho

कठोर

kaṭhora

(a.)

cruel

कण्ठोष्ठम्

kaṇṭhoṣṭham

(n.)

guttural-labial

ड ड ड ड ड

2 →
↓1

ḍa

डा डा डा डा डा

ḍā

डि डि डि डि डि डि

ḍi

पीडित

pīḍita

(a.)

tormented

डी डी डी डी डी डी

ḍī

डीनम्

ḍīnam

(n.)

flight

ढ ढ ढ ढ ढ

2 → ↓1

ḍha

ढक्का — ḍhakkā (f.) drum

मूढ — mūḍha (a.) deluded

ढि ढि ढि ढि ढि ढि

ḍhi

रूढिः

rūḍhiḥ

(f.)

well-known meaning

ण ण ण ण ण

ṇa

गुणः gunaḥ (m.) quality

पूर्णम् pūrṇam (n.) fullness

णा णा णा णा णा

ṇā

तृष्णा tṛṣṇā (f.) thirst

वीणा vīṇā (f.) a musical instrument

णि णि णि णि णि

ṇi

पाणिः pāṇiḥ (m.) hand

वारुणिः vāruṇiḥ (m.) name of a sage

णु णु णु णु णु

ṇu

अणुः aṇuḥ (m.) atom

त त त त त

ta

तत्त्वम् tattvam (n.) truth

तर्कः tarkaḥ (m.) logic

ता ता ता ता ता

tā

तापः tāpaḥ (m.) heat

तारका tārakā (f.) star

ति ति ति ति ति

ti

तितिक्षा titikṣā (f.) endurance

तिमिरः timiraḥ (m.) darkness

ती ती ती ती ती

tī

तीरम् tīram (n.) shore

तीर्थम् tīrtham (n.) holy place

तु तु तु तु तु

tu

तुला   तुष्ट
tulā   tuṣṭa
(f.)   (a.)
balance pleased

तू तू तू तू तू

tū

तूष्णीम् तूर्णम्
tūṣṇīm tūrṇam
(ind.)   (ind.)
silently quickly

तृ तृ तृ तृ तृ

tṛ

तृणम्   तृतीय
tṛṇam   tṛtīya
(n.)   (a.)
grass   third

तॄ तॄ तॄ तॄ तॄ

tṝ

ते ते ते ते ते

te

तेजः tejaḥ (n.) light

तेजोमय tejomaya (a.) brilliant

तै तै तै तै तै

tai

तैलम् tailam (n.) oil

हितैषी hitaiṣī (m.) well wisher

तो तो तो तो तो

to

तोयम् toyam (n.) water

तोषः toṣaḥ (m.) satisfaction

तौ तौ तौ तौ तौ

tau

तौलम् taulam (n.) balance

तौल्यम् taulyam (n.) equality

थ थ थ थ थ

tha

मथनम्
mathanam
(n.)
churning

प्रथम
prathama
(a.)
first

था था था था था

thā

तथा
tathā
(ind.)
in that manner

अवस्था
avasthā
(f.)
state

थि थि थि थि थि

thi

तिथिः
tithiḥ
(m.)
lunar day

अतिथिः
atithiḥ
(m.)
guest

थी थी थी थी थी

thī

अर्थी
arthī
(m.)
one who desires

चतुर्थी
caturthī
(f.)
fourth

थु थु थु थु थु

thu

मिथुनम् वेपथुः

mithunam vepathuḥ

(n.) (m.)

pair trembling

थू थू थू थू थू

thū

स्थूल

sthūla

(a.)

gross

थे थे थे थे थे

the

स्थेमा

sthemā

(m.)

firmness

थै थै थै थै थै

thai

स्थैर्यम्

sthairyam

(n.)

stability

थो थो थो थो थो

tho

अथो

atho

(ind.)

now

थौ थौ थौ थौ थौ

thau

स्थौल्यम्

sthaulyam

(n.)

bulkiness

2 → ↓1

द द द द द

da

दशम — daśama (a.) tenth

दया — dayā (f.) compassion

दा दा दा दा दा

dā

दानम् — dānam (n.) giving

दारु — dāru (n.) wood

दि दि दि दि दि

di

दिनम्   दिश्
dinam   diś
(n.)   (f.)
day   direction

दी दी दी दी दी

dī

दीपः   दीर्घ
dīpaḥ   dīrgha
(m.)   (a.)
lamp   long

दु दु दु दु दु

du

दुरित   दुर्गा
durita   durgā
(a.)   (f.)
discomfort   name of a
goddess

दू दू दू दू दू

dū

दूरम्   दूषणम्
dūram   dūṣaṇam
(ind.)   (n.)
far   blemish

दृ दृ दृ दृ दृ

dṛ

दृढ dṛḍha (a.) firm

दृष्टिः dṛṣṭiḥ (f.) vision

दे दे दे दे दे

de

देवता devatā (f.) god

देहः dehaḥ (m.) body

दो दो दो दो दो

do

दोषः doṣaḥ (m.) fault

दोहनम् dohanam (n.) milking

दौ दौ दौ दौ दौ

dau

दौर्भाग्यम् daurbhāgyam (n.) ill-luck

दौहित्रः dauhitraḥ (m.) daughter's son

ध

dha

धनम्
dhanam
(n.)
wealth

धर्मः
dharmaḥ
(m.)
duty

धा

dha

धारा
dhārā
(f.)
stream

धान्यम्
dhānyam
(n.)
grain

धि

dhi

विधिः
vidhiḥ
(m.)
order

उपाधिः
upādhiḥ
(m.)
condition

धी

dhī

धीः
dhīḥ
(f.)
intellect

धीर
dhīra
(a.)
intelligent

धु धु धु धु धु धु

dhu

अधुना साधु

adhunā sādhu

(ind.) now

(a.) excellent

धू धू धू धू धू धू

dhū

धूपः धूमः

dhūpaḥ dhūmaḥ

(m.) incense

(m.) smoke

धृ धृ धृ धृ धृ धृ

dhṛ

धृतिः अवधृत

dhṛtiḥ avadhṛta

(f.) firmness

(a.) determined

धॄ धॄ धॄ धॄ धॄ धॄ

dhṝ

धे धे धे धे धे

dhe

धेनुः

dhenuḥ

(f.)

cow

धै धै धै धै धै

dhai

धैर्यम्

dhairyam

(n.)

courage

धो धो धो धो धो

dho

अधोमुख

adhomukha

(a.)

facing downward

धौ धौ धौ धौ धौ

dhau

धौत

dhauta

(a.)

washed

न

na

नमः नभः

namaḥ nabhaḥ

(ind.) (n.)

salutation sky

ना

nā

नाटकः नागः

nāṭakaḥ nāgaḥ

(m.) (m.)

actor cobra

नि

ni

नियमः निशा

niyamaḥ niśā

(m.) (f.)

regulation night

नी

nī

नील नीडम्

nīla nīḍam

(a.) (n.)

blue nest

नु नु नु नु नु

nu

धनुः dhanuḥ (n.) bow

जानु jānu (n.) knee

नू नू नू नू नू

nū

नूतन nūtana (a.) new

नूनम् nūnam (ind.) surely

नृ नृ नृ नृ नृ

nṛ

नृपः nṛpaḥ (m.) king

नृत्यम् nṛtyam (n.) dance

नॄ नॄ नॄ नॄ नॄ

nṝ

ने ने ने ने ने

ne

नेत्रम् नेता

netram (n.) eye

netā (m.) leader

नै नै नै नै नै

nai

नैसर्गिक नैवेद्यम्

naisargika (a.) natural

naivedyam (n.) offering

नो नो नो नो नो

no

नो

no (ind.) no

नौ नौ नौ नौ नौ

nau

नौः नौका

nauḥ (f.) boat

naukā (f.) boat

प पपपपप

pa

पदम्   परम

padam   parama
(n.)   (a.)
foot   best

पा पापापापा

pā

पालः   पाठः

pālaḥ   pāṭhaḥ
(m.)   (m.)
protector study

पि पिपिपिपि

pi

पिपासा   पिता

pipāsā   pitā
(f.)   (m.)
thirst   father

पी पीपीपीपी

pī

पीत   पीडा

pīta   pīḍā
(a.)   (f.)
yellow   pain

पु पु पु पु पु

pu

पुनः punaḥ (ind.) again

पुण्यम् puṇyam (n.) result of righteous action

पू पू पू पू पू

pū

पूजा pūjā (f.) worship

पूर्वम् pūrvam (ind.) before

पृ पृ पृ पृ पृ

pṛ

पृथिवी pṛthivī (f.) earth

पृष्ठतः pṛṣṭhataḥ (ind.) behind

पे पे पे पे पे

pe

पेयम् peyam (n.) drink

पेषणम् peṣaṇam (n.) grinding

पो पो पो पो पो

po

पोषणम् अपोहनम्

poṣaṇam (n.) nourishing

apohanam (n.) forgetfulness

पौ पौ पौ पौ पौ

pau

पौत्रः पौरुषेय

pautraḥ (m.) grandson

pauruṣeya (a.) made by man

फ फ फ फ फ

4 1 2 3

pha

फलम् फल्गु

phalam (n.) fruit

phalgu (a.) useless

फि फि फि फि फि

phi

फु फु फु फु फु

phu

फुल्ल
phulla
(a.)
open

फे फे फे फे फे

phe

फेणः
pheṇaḥ
(m.)
foam

ब ब ब ब ब

4 1 2 3

ba

बहिः
bahiḥ
(ind.)
outside

बलम्
balam
(n.)
power

बा बा बा बा बा

bā

बालः
bālaḥ
(m.)
boy

बाहुः
bāhuḥ
(m.)
arm

बि बि बि बि बि बि

bi

बिम्बः bimbaḥ (m.) image

बिन्दुः binduḥ (m.) drop

बी बी बी बी बी बी

bī

बीजम् bījam (n.) seed

बु बु बु बु बु बु

bu

बुद्धिः buddhiḥ (f.) intellect

बुभुक्षुः bubhukṣuḥ (m.) one who is hungry

बू बू बू बू बू बू

bū

ताम्बूलम् tāmbūlam (n.) betel leaf

बृ बृ बृ बृ बृ

bṛ

बृहत्

bṛhat

(a.)

big

बे बे बे बे बे

be

कुबेरः

kuberaḥ

(m.)

name of a devatā

बो बो बो बो बो

bo

बोधनम्

bodhanam

(n.)

knowledge

बौ बौ बौ बौ बौ

bau

बौद्धः

bauddhaḥ

(m.)

buddhist

भ भ भ भ भ

bha

भजनम्	भवः
bhajanam	bhavaḥ
(n.)	(m.)
worship	being

भा भा भा भा भा

bha

भाषा	भारतः
bhāṣā	bhārataḥ
(f.)	(m.)
language	India

भि भि भि भि भि

bhi

भिक्षा	भिन्न
bhikṣā	bhinna
(f.)	(a.)
taking of alms	different

भी भी भी भी भी

bhī

भीतिः	भीषा
bhītiḥ	bhīṣā
(f.)	(f.)
fear	fear

भु भु भु भु भु

bhu

भुक्तिः bhuktiḥ (f.) enjoyment

भुजगः bhujagaḥ (m.) snake

भू भू भू भू भू

bhū

भूः bhūḥ (f.) earth

भूत bhūta (a.) past

भृ भृ भृ भृ भृ

bhṛ

भृगुः bhṛguḥ (m.) name of a sage

भृशम् bhṛśam (ind.) intensely

भॄ भॄ भॄ भॄ भॄ

bhṝ

भे भे भे भे भे

bhe

भेदः bhedaḥ (m.) difference

भेदकः bhedakaḥ (m.) separator

भै भै भै भै भै

bhai

भैरवी bhairavī (f.) Durgā

भो भो भो भो भो

bho

भोजनम् bhojanam (n.) food

भोक्ता bhoktā (m.) experiencer

भौ भौ भौ भौ भौ

bhau

भौतिक bhautika (a.) elemental

भौम bhauma (a.) earthly

म म म म म

ma

मतिः matiḥ (f.) intellect

मनः manaḥ (n.) mind

मा मा मा मा मा

mā

माता mātā (f.) mother

मार्गः mārgaḥ (m.) way

मि मि मि मि मि

mi

मित्रम् mitram (n.) friend

मिथ्या mithyā (ind.) falsely

मी मी मी मी मी

mī

मीनः mīnaḥ (m.) fish

मीमांसा mīmāṁsā (f.) analysis

मु मु मु मु मु

mu

मुखः mukhaḥ (m.) face

मुनिः muniḥ (m.) wise person

मू मू मू मू मू

mū

मूलम् mūlam (n.) root

मूर्तिः mūrtiḥ (f.) form

मृ मृ मृ मृ मृ

mṛ

मृगः mṛgaḥ (m.) deer

मृत्युः mṛtyuḥ (m.) death

मॄ मॄ मॄ मॄ मॄ

mṝ

मे मे मे मे मे

me

मेघः meghaḥ (m.) cloud

मेधा medhā (f.) intellect

मै मै मै मै मै

mai

मैत्रम् maitram (n.) friendship

मो मो मो मो मो

mo

मोक्षः mokṣaḥ (m.) liberation

मोहः mohaḥ (m.) confusion

मौ मौ मौ मौ मौ

mau

मौनम् maunam (n.) silence

मौलिः mauliḥ (m.) head

य य य य य

ya

यशः
yaśaḥ
(n.)
fame

यथा
yathā
(ind.)
in which manner

या या या या या

yā

यागः
yāgaḥ
(m.)
ritual

यात्रा
yātrā
(f.)
journey

यि यि यि यि यि

yi

नैयायिकः
naiyāyikaḥ
(m.)
logician

यी यी यी यी यी

yī

मायी
māyī
(m.)
one who has māyā

मैत्रेयी
maitreyī
(f.)
name of a wife of yājñavalkya

यु यु यु यु यु

yu

युगः
yugaḥ
(m.)
cycle of time

युयुत्सुः
yuyutsuḥ
(m.)
one who desires to fight

यू यू यू यू यू

yū

यूपः
yūpaḥ
(m.)
sacrificial post

यूतिः
yūtiḥ
(f.)
union

यृ यृ यृ यृ यृ

yṛ

व्यृद्धिः
vyṛddhiḥ
(f.)
decline

ये ये ये ये ये

ye

प्रायेण
prāyeṇa
(ind.)
generally

यो यो यो यो यो

yo

योगः yogaḥ (m.) union

योनिः yoniḥ (m.) origin

यौ यौ यौ यौ यौ

yau

यौगिक yaugika (a.) derivative

यौवनम् yauvanam (n.) youth

र र र र र

2 →
↓1

ra

रतिः ratiḥ (f.) pleasure

रथः rathaḥ (m.) chariot

रा रा रा रा रा

rā

राजा rājā (m.) king

रागः rāgaḥ (m.) passion

रि रि रि रि रि रि

ri

रिपुः	वारि
ripuḥ	vāri
(m.)	(n.)
enemy	water

री री री री री री

rī

रीतिः	शरीरम्
rītiḥ	śarīram
(f.)	(n.)
style	body

रु रु रु रु रु

ru

रुचिः	तरुः
ruciḥ	taruḥ
(f.)	(m.)
taste	tree

रू रू रू रू रू

rū

रूपम्	रूढिः
rūpam	rūḍhiḥ
(n.)	(f.)
form	custom

ॠ ॠ ॠ ॠ ॠ

rṝ

रे रे रे रे रे

re

रेखा rekhā (f.) line

रेफः rephaḥ (m.) r-sound

रै रै रै रै रै

rai

रैः raiḥ (m.) wealth

रो रो रो रो रो

ro

रोगः rogaḥ (m.) disease

रोचन rocana (a.) bright

ल ल ल ल ल

la

लता — latā (f.) creeper

लयः — layaḥ (m.) absorption

ला ला ला ला ला

lā

लाभः — lābhaḥ (m.) gain

ललाटः — lalāṭaḥ (m.) forehead

लि लि लि लि लि

li

लिखनम् — likhanam (n.) writing

लिपिः — lipiḥ (f.) script

ली ली ली ली ली

lī

लीन — līna (a.) absorbed

लीला — līlā (f.) sport

लु लु लु लु लु

lu

लुप्त
lupta
(a.)
disappeared

खलु
khalu
(ind.)
indeed

लू लू लू लू लू

lū

लूता
lūtā
(m.)
spider

ले ले ले ले ले

le

लेखा
lekhā
(f.)
line

लेपनम्
lepanam
(n.)
ointment

लै लै लै लै लै

lai

लो लो लो लो लो

lo

लोकः लोपः

lokaḥ lopaḥ

(m.) world

(m.) disappearance

लौ लौ लौ लौ लौ

lau

लौकिक

laukika

(a.) worldly

व व व व व

3 1 2

va

वनम् वचः

vanam vacaḥ

(n.) forest

(n.) word

वा वा वा वा वा

vā

वाक् वादः

vāk vādaḥ

(f.) word

(m.) discussion

वि वि वि वि वि

vi _____

विरागः विनयः

virāgaḥ vinayaḥ
(m.) (m.)
dispassion modesty

वी वी वी वी वी

vī _____

वीरः वीर्यम्

vīraḥ vīryam
(m.) (n.)
hero strength

वृ वृ वृ वृ वृ

vṛ _____

वृषभः वृकः

vṛṣabhaḥ vṛkaḥ
(m.) (m.)
bull wolf

वॄ वॄ वॄ वॄ वॄ

vṝ _____

वे वे वे वे वे

ve

वेदः vedaḥ (m.) the Veda

वेधाः vedhāḥ (m.) brahmājī

वै वै वै वै वै

vai

वैदिकः vaidikaḥ (m.) one who follows the Veda

वैभवम् vaibhavam (n.) greatness

वो वो वो वो वो

vo

वोढा voḍhā (m.) porter

वौ वौ वौ वौ वौ

vau

वौषट् vauṣaṭ (ind.) exclamation in offering

श श श श श

śa

शमः — śamaḥ (m.) calmness

शयनम् — śayanam (n.) sleeping

शा शा शा शा शा

śā

शाला — śālā (f.) hall

शासनम् — śāsanam (n.) order

शि शि शि शि शि

śi

शिवः — śivaḥ (m.) name of god

शिरः — śiraḥ (n.) head

शी शी शी शी शी

śī

शीलम् — śīlam (n.) character

शीत — śīta (a.) cold

शु शु शु शु शु

śu

शुभ
śubha
(a.)
auspicious

शुचिः
śuciḥ
(m.)
purity

शू शू शू शू शू

śū

शूर
śūra
(a.)
brave

शून्य
śūnya
(a.)
empty

शृ शृ शृ शृ शृ

śṛ

शृगालः
śṛgālaḥ
(m.)
jackal

शॄ शॄ शॄ शॄ शॄ

śṝ

शे शे शे शे शे

śe

शेखरः śekharaḥ (m.) crest

शेषः śeṣaḥ (m.) remaining

शै शै शै शै शै

śai

शैत्यम् śaityam (n.) coldness

शो शो शो शो शो

śo

शोकः śokaḥ (m.) sorrow

शोषः śoṣaḥ (m.) dryness

शौ शौ शौ शौ शौ

śau

शौर्यम् śauryam (n.) strength

ष

ṣa

विषयः
viṣayaḥ
(m.)
subject

दोषः
doṣaḥ
(m.)
fault

षा

ṣā

तुषारः
tuṣāraḥ
(m.)
snow

मनीषा
manīṣā
(f.)
desire

षि

ṣi

इषिका
iṣikā
(f.)
bush

ऋषिः
ṛṣiḥ
(m.)
sage

षी

ṣī

हृषीकम्
hṛṣīkam
(n.)
sense organ

षु षु षु षु षु

ṣu

इषुः
iṣuḥ
(m.)
arrow

चिकीर्षुः
cikīrṣuḥ
(m.)
one who desires to do

षू षू षू षू षू

ṣū

विषूचिः
viṣūciḥ
(m.)
mind

निषूदनम्
niṣūdanam
(n.)
one who kills

षे षे षे षे षे

ṣe

अभिषेकः
abhiṣekaḥ
(m.)
anointing

निषेधः
niṣedhaḥ
(m.)
prohibition

षो षो षो षो षो

ṣo

षोडश
ṣoḍaśa
(a.)
sixteenth

षोढा
ṣoḍhā
(ind.)
in six ways

स स स स स

sa

सकृत्
sakṛt
(ind.)
once

सदृश
sadṛśa
(a.)
similar

सा सा सा सा सा

sā

सारः
sāraḥ
(m.)
essence

साधनम्
sādhanam
(n.)
means

सि सि सि सि सि

si

सिंहः
siṁhaḥ
(m.)
lion

असिः
asiḥ
(m.)
sword

सी सी सी सी सी

sī

सीता
sītā
(f.)
name of the wife of Rāma

सरसी
sarasī
(f.)
lake

सु सु सु सु सु

su

सुतः sutaḥ (m.) son

सुरः suraḥ (m.) god

सू सू सू सू सू

sū

सूत्रम् sūtram (n.) thread

असूया asūyā (f.) envy

सृ सृ सृ सृ सृ

sṛ

सृष्टिः sṛṣṭiḥ (f.) creation

प्रसृत prasṛta (a.) extended

से से से से से

se

सेतुः setuḥ (m.) bridge

सेवा sevā (f.) service

सो सो सो सो सो

so

सोमः somaḥ (m.) moon

सोढ soḍha (a.) endured

सौ सौ सौ सौ सौ

sau

सौभाग्यम् saubhāgyam (n.) good fortune

ह ह ह ह ह

3 1 2

ha

हरिः hariḥ (m.) name of lord

हनुः hanuḥ (m.) jaw

हा हा हा हा हा

hā

हासः hāsaḥ (m.) laughter

विहारः vihāraḥ (m.) sporting ground

हि

hi

हितम् hitam (n.) welfare

हिमम् himam (n.) snow

ही

hī

हीन hīna (a.) low

मही mahī (f.) earth

हु

hu

हुतम् hutam (n.) oblation

बहु bahu (a.) many

हू

hū

आहूतिः āhūtiḥ (f.) invoking

हूहूः hūhūḥ (m.) name of a celestial

हृ हृ हृ हृ हृ

hṛ

हृदयम् hṛdayam (n.) heart

हृषीकम् hṛṣīkam (n.) sense organ

हे हे हे हे हे

he

हेतुः hetuḥ (m.) cause

हेमन्तः hemantaḥ (m.) winter

है है है है है

hai

हैमवती haimavatī (f.) Pārvatī

हैतुक haituka (a.) causal

हो हो हो हो हो

ho

होमः homaḥ (m.) fire ritual

होता hotā (m.) priest

Printed in Great Britain
by Amazon

25949970R00046